Emily's
Everyday Manners

Emily Post

Emily's Everyday Manners

by PEGGY POST &
CINDY POST SENNING, Ed.D.

illustrated by STEVE BJÖRKMAN

Collins
An Imprint of HarperCollins Publishers

Collins is an imprint of HarperCollins Publishers.
Emily's Everyday Manners
Text copyright © 2006 by Peggy Post and Cindy Post Senning
Illustrations copyright © 2006 by Steve Björkman
Manufactured in China.

Library of Congress Cataloging-in-Publication Data
Post, Peggy.
    Emily's everyday manners / by Peggy Post and Cindy Post Senning ; illustrated by
Steve Björkman.— 1st ed.
        p.   cm.
    ISBN-10: 0-06-076174-1 (trade bdg.) — ISBN-13: 978-0-06-076174-5 (trade bdg.)
    ISBN-10: 0-06-076177-6 (lib. bdg.) — ISBN-13: 978-0-06-076177-6 (lib. bdg.)
    1. Etiquette for children and teenagers. I. Title: Emily's everyday manners. II. Title:
Everyday manners. III. Senning, Cindy Post. IV. Title.
BJ1857.C5P63 2006   2005020601
395.1'22-dc22
Typography by Jeanne L. Hogle
13 SCP 10 9 8 7 6 5
❖
First Edition

We dedicate this book to all kids everywhere! And to Emily Post, whose timeless wisdom serves as the basis for this book.
—P.P. and C.P.S.

To Mom—"Thank you" for teaching me to say "please."
—S.B.

Emily and Ethan are best friends.
They like to do everything together.
They go to school together.
They eat lunch together.
They play together.

Emily and Ethan love their family and friends.
They want them to feel good.

Here are your
glasses, Granny.

So they do kind things for others and
use good manners every day.

Good manners take practice. Sometimes Emily and Ethan forget. But they never give up trying!

Did you know that certain words can make people feel happy, just like magic?

Emily does.

EMILY'S MAGIC WORDS

Emily and Ethan use manners every day

with their families,

their friends,

and everyone they meet.

Some manners get used a lot.

Some manners get used only once or twice.

Some manners get used on special occasions, like today. Emily and Ethan are going to a birthday party!

Emily and Ethan use good table manners whether they are eating at home or they are eating out.

What a polite, grown-up girl!

USE THE RIGHT UTENSILS FOR THE FOOD

Using good manners is more than remembering magic words and table manners. It is being helpful, kind, and friendly.

NOTE HOW HANDY THAT NAPKIN IS. . . .

Good manners are very important when you go to school.

Next time, it's your turn to go first, Ethan. Be patient while waiting in line.

Manners help Ethan and Emily get along with the grown-ups there.

They help Ethan and Emily make friends and get along with the other children.

And manners help them keep friends too.
When Emily has friends over, she's the *host*.

When Ethan goes to Sam's house, he is the *guest*.

There are different manners for different places:

Go Tigers!!!

There is a time to yell,

Look at this cute
picture of a monkey!

a time to talk quietly,

a time not to talk at all.

...And I don't have to tell you not to do this...

Emily's Don'ts

whaa-hooo!

What you say can make others feel good.

When you are not sure what to do,

be respectful,

be considerate,

AFTERWORD FOR ADULTS

Etiquette is more than just manners! All the manners mentioned in this book are rooted in three fundamental principles: respect, consideration, and honesty. As your children learn manners, it is essential that they also learn these principles, for the manners by themselves are hollow rules to be memorized and soon forgotten.

Children learn from the adults around them. Treat children with respect and they will learn self-respect and to respect others. Treat them with consideration and they will learn to be considerate of others. Always be honest in what you do and say, and they will learn to be honest in all they do and say.

Manners are tools you give your children to help them navigate the complexities of social interaction. As with any tool, it takes practice to learn to use manners correctly. And then it takes repetition to develop those habits of use that will make them second nature. Play manners with your children. Practice handshakes. Role-play introductions. Have parties with dolls and stuffed animals. Develop secret signals to remember manners you're working on. Praise your children when they get it right. Gently remind them when they don't. Learn what you can expect and then expect it.

And, finally, we would like to remind you of the Golden Rule of Parenting: Always behave the way you want your children to behave. They will learn the most from watching you. If you tell them to do one thing and then you do another, they will do what you do, not what you say. Respect them, show them what consideration is, and be honest. Then the manners you teach will be meaningful, and your children will take them to heart.